Glitter Glue the Slowly Sinking Idols

Glitter Glue the Slowly Sinking Idols

Chapbook by

Andrés Amitai Wilson

Cover by Shay Culligan
Cover image by Sharon McCutcheon

ISBN: 978-1-63980-090-2

Kelsay Books
502 South 1040 East, A-119
American Fork, Utah 84003
Kelsaybooks.com

Acknowledgments

The Pomona Valley Review 9*:* "Nazareth"

The Stonecoast Review: "Old Barn Road"

Kweli Journal: "Hattie May Parris"

Lucky Jefferson (3)*:* "Baba's *Asana*"

The Whirlwind Review: "Ghost Bike"

Artichoke Haircut: "Freiburg: from Wallace Stevens to Heidegger"

Danse Macabre: "Grace"

Mima'amakim: "Cozbi and Zimri"

Bird's Eye Review: "Jogging While Black"

The Prose: "Black Orpheus"

Contents

Nazareth (for Eden)

benedicta qui venit in nomine domini
["Blessed is *she* that comes in the name of the Father"]
—Dante, after John the Baptist

I.

To this city of rice and weddings,
overflowing like a toppled barrel
of pearls, we Jews ascend.

Driving up the mountain
that hovers over Galilee
like revelation, it seems
from the windows of
our puny Peugeot that
here, Jesus speaks
Arabic and wears
a *kaffiyah.*

II.

Pigeons flee the gait
of Eden—17 months quick,
lumbering through gardens
in slow-motion with seahorse
curls bouncing, with eyes
aflame.

She is curious, un-gated.
Eden tickles even the severest
cherubim to chuckles; she is endless
and intoxicating like the first
bedouin's desert dream.

III.

The *hortus conclusus:* a steepled square
where pilgrims meet—nuns and
African executives—under an English
sign that reads, "Know the Truth of Islam,"
with Aladdin's golden lamp in the bottom
corner and a number to call. Here, the old
men tell stories from twisted teeth
over boards of backgammon. Here,
another mother leans to bless
our child in a mythic language

we don't understand; she places
her hands upon each of Eden's
chrysanthemum cheeks and incants
some arid mantra of Muhammad
(or the Muses) above these stones
and blossoms quarried
to cities. Here, the world
is constructed through
words like a prophecy.

IV.

When the actual Messiah
comes to these hills of holy
fire, she will don a pink
tutu with ruffles that crest
like waves, her pupils ever
expanding outward

from desert sands like
another Big
Bang.

When the actual Messiah
comes, the parchments
of prophecy will be doused
in glitter glue and sparkles, then
crumpled and tossed to the alley,
like any other good metaphor
once the truth it signifies
is understood.

Old Barn Road (or "As Antiquated as Alchemy")

She lived on Old Barn Road
in the cotton-candy farmhouse
where unicorns would graze.
She lived in the gossamer
where Paul Revere rode—black
shutters not yet chipping, chicken
coops quiet as dreamed winter
rain.

She'd knit, yoke rainbows
with yarn, watch the still
handsome men on game shows,
ensconced within eight-millimeter eyelashes.

She'd tap the Lincoln's steering wheel to Woody Herman,
to Duke, to Benny, to the five-part harmony of Jesus horns.

I often visit memories in which I am blooming and scared
of beasties. Often I smell the woodstove music of the hearth
while she inoculates dragons. She forages, finds raspberries,
furry and overflowing like moksha cornucopias,
gigantic grapes, and strawberries—that presage my future wife.

I learn about etiquette, the merits of "thank you," how smiling is
the face of God. In exchange, I recount the girls whose hair
summered, or I trip over fingers full of wooden chords, and she
waves nods like a wand—my fairy godmother on Old Barn Road.

She lived on Old Barn Road,
a thorn bush away from Route 3,
in that rickety barn as overgrown
and antiquated

as alchemy.

A Portrait of Hattie May Parris
(an Ancestor Poem)

Hattie May Parris wears the white
dress of silent screens, her eyes
implode event horizons, her skin
gleams the Smith and Wessons
of dueling suitors in unknown
meadows.

In the one picture we have
of her—faded and revered like
a wedding dress from another century, Hattie May Parris
holds the pink roses of posterity
without a vase to contain them. The hand-painted
flowers are the only color here,
overflowing like twins in a womb
within this shot of black
and white, as distinct and unutterable
as the Tao.

Hattie May Parris smiles
with my grandmother's honey
face—or is it my mother's?—
the long, dark-amber jaw of the bald
monk who knows her own face
before her grandparents were
born, but Hattie May Parris'
own hair has been burned straight
by lye, its rich black
webs enshroud the dark orb like
the perfumed flesh of some
Pharaoh's consort.

Hattie May Parris poses before the coop
where Nana learned to chop the heads
off chickens and cried immediately after
as the dumb birds hopped their last Lindy Hop
into feathered nothingness.

Why did Hattie May Parris venture
here from the Fundy Bay—doused
in Micmac blood, clothed in African
nightmares—back to the shaded
and Puritanical land where I
doubt she was ever
welcome?

Baba's *Asana*

Man is all symmetrie,
Full of proportions, one limbe to another,
And all to all the world besides;
Each part may call the farthest brother,
For head with foot hath private amitie,
And both with moons and tides.
—From George Herbert's "Man"

His corduroyed knees
of falling leaves collapse
expertly on the bald
head that I like to rub
when we hug.

The old sergeant
rolls up and down
in his ancient fatigues
above the spotted kitchen rug
of Massachusetts dirt and
blood; Massachusetts that the natives
named "many mountains" and he was
nearly as native as they.

Already in his eighties, Baba asks
miniature me—perhaps four and
aflame—what I have eaten for breakfast
on an autumn morning of fuzzy
sweaters and talk-radio hustle.

While mother brews English
Breakfast then scurries off
to desks far away, Baba stays
to demonstrate what he learned
in India and Burma as the other GIs
went mad in opium clouds
or the laps of working women,

17

he stood as so many mountains; he
stood as warriors assembled, as heroes and their triumphant
Vedic dogs facing up and down on breath's resilient command.
His lungs and throat would surge full
of Earth-rumbling stardust,
then expel universes back
into the endless.

I doubt Baba ever
killed anyone over there
in World War II. They didn't let
most blacks kill—confining us
to the cornbread and the patriotic
pots and pans. Then, of course, there's that legend—
bitter as the alcohol that he had "never even
tried"—of being on leave in Georgia, already
a sergeant with a lapel full of supernova,
sitting arm in arm with Nana on a park bench
when the angry mouths drawled "no
coloreds" and tugged hard at the dark
matter around the stars and stripes.

In a new millennium that he
wouldn't see, where we lumber
like plastic zombies through
the digital, I—sort of a man now—
roll my spine across floors
and remember.

I have learned that this funny dance
of yolking the disparate
pieces of self to Self is called "yoga," that,

though words are but blurred signs, fingers
pointing to constellations, but not those shapes
themselves, that there are lots of long Sanskrit
scribbles that speak of motion, that yoga
itself is a dead metaphor, etymologically
related to other words that seek
for "to unify," but is only
known twisting bones
and wringing muscle and
and reaching down to earth,
but also up to the sky,
letting the breath
and the heart
do the work.

But on those mornings, I only thought of Baba
doing his weird exercises on the floor—
an old man, blacker than event
horizons—not twisting like an ancient,
but smiling from the black
face of my America.

Grace (an elegy for Jeff Buckley)

That river is still but as green as then,
Flowing past branches and twisted in knots,
Dampening with touch and touching each end,
But moving along and twisting its bends.
And on that night, they say you'd sunk,
While wading with a case of truth,
And met your maker like a monk,
Who'd cleared his mind of all.
At first I wished I'd been there,
To keep you buoyant and alive
So you could spread your supple voice
And let it echo, soar, and writhe.
But prophets only live to die
As songs and lyrics live and thrive

The Hebrew Home for the Aged

Et nul ne vous salue, étranges destinées!
Débris d'humanité pour l'éternité mûrs!
—Charles Baudelaire, "Les petites vielles," IV
[And no one greets you, strange destinies!/ Human debris ripe for eternity!]

We volunteered,
armed with Ivy-League degrees
and Liberalism, to combat the clang of death's
trays of gelatin and pills
in paper cups emblazoned with long numbers,
to bring *shalom* to the forgotten
grandmothers of Manhattan.

We, the future rabbis, the keepers
of quaint Semitic laws,
with the wave of name-badge wands
became chaplains wearing knit *kippahs* atop
balding heads, heads spinning with
words and words and Bibles full of words.

But here, we had to listen—listen
on the dementia floor for which the elevator
required a code—to the one-eyed socialite
who had won a bet on the Brown Bomber
at Madison Square Garden, and after
three minutes of sweet speech would begin
to address me as if I were the unfaithful
husband who had stolen her other eye, and

we would listen to the Southern songs of Mattie
in the stroke unit who would warn me about the dangers
of salt and extol the caress of green liniments,
or listen to Rose whose son was always supposed to
visit but never did—our Rose, with the voice as

faint as wisdom, a voice for which I'd have to
draw closer or else it would be drowned
in antiseptic and screams from the hallway.

At the Hebrew Home, there were grandfathers, too,
equally forgotten like the antiquated newspaper headlines that line
boxes of the fragile—Donald, who was a paratrooper
in Vietnam and now watched Fox News,
lamented the loss of America. Donald said he
was getting out any day now, but the nurses
knew nothing about that; he had no place to go,
so he opted instead for a third stroke. The last time
I saw him, he squeezed my hand and blinked Empire-
State eyes from a mash-potato face.

We volunteered here at the Hebrew Home
where words run out but something else
must be offered—a handshake, a song,
a smile; anything but a Bible.

Ghost Bike

haunts
my every morning,
garbed in the off-
white hymns,
in the traffic-light
rhythms.

Its front tire is flat;
its rear, floating.
Both rest in the
indefinite, in the spaces,
the serrated links
between locks,
the messy threads
of place and nowhere.

Ghost Bike withers
petals, autumns
songs to rusty manacles,
to mangled spokes,
yet new flowers
appear weekly—as if left by storks
or bees who clothe her
in buzzing rainbows
or winds
of orchards
again.

Some days
I think to offer
my own bouquet—
vigorous, erect—

a moveable garden
of aphids, on a
valley morning
when all dirges
are sung
and I can imagine
my own wheels
going flat.

But today's the traffic
and it spins as a wheel,
revolving unnoticed
into never
again.

Yoga Studio

Between four walls
inside brownstone building
we wind bodies into
eagles, into dogs, into sphinxes,
into warriors, with the vision
of mountains, sweating oceans
as the breath crests and breaks.

Of course, there are Sanskrit names
for all this play, that we have come to recognize,
but mainly we know shapes:
bodies, angles. we remember how it feels
in the skin, in the muscles, down to the bones–
the fusing of shoulders and back, the contraction
of quads and calves; the twists into ribs and organs;
the green and blue waves of tattoos
expanding over skin like continents
stretched across the roundness of the globe,
not interrupted by waters dammed but flowing

in and out of
all.

Cozbi and Zimri (after Numbers 25)

A sharp removal: triceps return flesh,
Burgundy triangle lance dances slow
Above the broken vessels—seeping thresh.
Phineas ruffles priestly brow, eyes low.

How can those holy fingers elevate
After slicing through missteps of the dead?
Cozbi, a woman who germinates bait,
Easily bitten off by the prince, red—

Weak. Night quivers like a bonfire's embers.
Broken bottles, casks, grapes in the dirt,
Swallowed by earth, preserved in the amber—
Like mosquitoes; ink on parchment; long skirts?
Phineas, we dance through desert, lovesick—
Our shipwrecked race. Why a reward for this?

Freiburg: from Wallace Stevens to Heidegger

The streets are haunted
by hushed, rainbow years.
None are green, as the colorblind
Black Forest, or blue as a *sosie* of the
sky, or yellow like an aching fever,
or purple the Dreisam's royal sigh.
None of them are gauche,
with sunflowers creeping over fences;
just cobblestone, poking underfoot.
Who would dream of indignant phantoms
pouring forth like merlot from a
cracked bottle? Only here
and there, a monument,
an inscription,
inscrutable,
carved at the bottom
of some well
out of
view.

Jogging while Black

I open my hand
to prove I bear no knife—
with which I would disembowel your lilies
though I certainly be black,
on this black, black night.

I cross the street
to attest I stalk you not,
tracked and trapped like a lion
as my foot taps
the setting asphalt.

I, see two waves cresting into each other;
You…perhaps an Other…

On the prowl.

Black Orpheus

After Carnaval, he lost
Eurydice in crests
of dissonance–the Sisyphus
glissando, the cyclical slipping
back.
The master
of bossa, his blue
      crime was merely
                      a backward glance.

Erik (for the Phantom of the Opera)

With Carnaval about to start,
at last, I'll don my cracking mask,
and split the concrete breast of Styx—
and part the Hades I call home.
The phantom is a man again;
a man, who wields the frozen fire,
and sings the songs of Adam's sons,
and drinks the wine that Noah drank.
Christine! I was your black-caped god,
an Orphic genie in the wings,
the fiddler plucking broken strings
for every abject *shtetl* soul.
(I'd crescent to the quasar—
invisible in pizzicato—
the slow echoes of clouds;
I was prelapsarian honey.
I was wheat spun to gold.)
But once unmasked, what more is left,
but scars of shrieks, but shards of pluck,
but melting truth, but creeping death
and sirens humming secret
doom?

Zen on Main Street

The wall counts breath
in white squares of tile,
in black squares of tile,
in mortar mind.

Toes graze cushion,
Knees root buckwheat.
Wooden Buddha flickers
In winter flames and wick.

Every few minutes—
The chime begins…
The chime begins…
The chime begins…

and shadows flicker
across main street.

Do they see us dancing
from the windows—
fist to solar plexus,
feet, gliding as ghosts
above main street?

Do they feel us sensing them
with feet tucked beneath bottoms,
pelvis, coronary throne,
encircling the belly?
The *hara* quickens.
Then, squeezes out
death.

In fact, who is this "they?"
And, further, who is this "us?"
And who is "who?"
And what is "what?

About the Author

Andrés Amitai Wilson currently serves on the English faculty at the Roxbury Latin School in Boston, where he teaches English, music, and yoga. He is also a busy session and touring guitarist with many recordings and performance credits, in genres from hip-hop to jazz and everything in between. Andrés holds a Ph.D. in Comparative Literature from the University of Massachusetts, Amherst, and has also earned degrees from Columbia University and the Berklee College of Music. When not making music, reading, or writing, he can usually be found running around in the woods with his three children, practicing yoga, or riding his bicycle.

www.ingramcontent.com/pod-product-compliance
Lightning Source LLC
Chambersburg PA
CBHW031155090426
42738CB00008B/1350